Walking with
Wisdom

Nan C. Merrill

Lantern Books • New York

A Division of Booklight, Inc.

2009
Lantern Books
128 Second Place
Brooklyn, NY 11231
www.lanternbooks.com

Cover photograph by Anne L. Strader © 2009

LIBRARY OF CONGRESS CATALOGING-IN-PUBLICATION DATA
Merrill, Nan C.
Walking with wisdom / Nan C. Merrill.
    p. cm.
  ISBN-13: 978-1-59056-143-0 (alk. paper)
  ISBN-10: 1-59056-143-0 (alk. paper)
  1. Wisdom. I. Title.
  BJ1595.M46 2009
  204'.32—dc22

                                        2009024006

A portion of the profits from this book will be donated to Friends of Silence and to the Guild for Spiritual Guidance, nonprofit organizations.

Acknowledgments

I WISH TO OFFER MY heartfelt gratitude to Alice O. Howell for her friendship, teachings, and patience as she introduced me to Sophia-Wisdom over the years. For as long as I have known her, Alice has embodied Wisdom and Sophia energy and, indeed, has received several Wisdom-awards. Her books, especially, *The Dove in the Stone,* a personal journey to Iona with her husband Walter, who also knew Sophia's energy, mischief, and delight, may give the reader an experience of living with Sophia.

My deep thanks to several other friends and colleagues, who helped and graciously supported me as I wrote *Walking with Wisdom:* Elaine Allistone, Nancy Bloomer, Renate Craine, Gay Grissom, Marc Legerton, Evander Lomke, Jo McClellan, Anne Strader, and Sally Woodhall. I will ever be grateful for all the members of the Guild for Spiritual Guidance, a two-year apprenticeship and growing community dedicated to the inward journey. The program continues to enhance my life more than I can express. To one and all, please know how much your willingness to walk in wisdom with me over the years means; it has made all the difference. "We are never alone," for I carry you in my heart with Love.

Walk with Wisdom...Live with wisdom.

Introduction

WISDOM IS A PRICELESS Treasure for all generations…a spirituality of relationships found in everyday life. She invites us to participate with Her in the Divine Dance of Life in a triune community: with others, with Creation, and with Love Consciousness. The meditations in *Walking with Wisdom* are reflections of Her gentle guidance and humble, awakening teachings of how we can live with more vibrancy, discernment, humility, and integrity; a life that transcends death and leads to our true Life in the unseen Realm of Love. She compares those who have awakened with the obstacles those who still sleep must face; who, like little children, believe that they can have whatever they want whenever they want it giving no mind to how it may affect others.

Inspired by and with some inclusions from the Apocryphal Book of Wisdom credited to Solomon, I was struck by the similarity to present-day conflicts over land and religion, power and greed. Wisdom has ever been needed and, all too often, ignored. Her teachings and guidance, which can awaken and uplift our consciousness, cannot be underestimated: the time has never been more crucial. The efficacy, one might even call it necessity, for times of silence, solitude, simplicity, and stillness, is paramount to Her. Wisdom knows the road to peace and harmony where balance is achieved, especially the balance of feminine and masculine energies. She honors the yearning of our souls for union with Wisdom and the Beloved, as well as the joy of conscious participation in loving and mutual service to Creation's well-being in the Divine Dance.

Somewhere in the process of writing, I was blessed with what seemed a great *aha*, perhaps shades of the obvious to others. While walking with Wisdom, I realized that I was experiencing two compatible, yet very different energies: Wisdom as masculine, Sophia as feminine. Questioning this from within, I understood that just as each one of us carries both the masculine and feminine energy, it made sense that Sophia and Wisdom are One in Being, Two in expression, and become a Trinity with each of us as we interact with them. This became even clearer to me in a dream that awakened me the night I completed the last meditation:

> *I was driving to some unknown place with an unknown passenger. Suddenly, I felt compelled to turn onto what I thought was a road to the left, realizing too late that it was almost a precipice. Other drivers lined up behind me and became impatient; I had to make a quick choice: Do I turn left and enter*

the garage to an institute for Learning?; or, do I continue to drive toward the precipice? I chose the precipice. The road was minimal and clouds enveloped the car; yet, the sky and invisible horizon seemed to be hiding a brilliant light that broke through the clouds from time to time. This road to nowhere seemed endless and the passenger was close to screaming. "No fear" soon became my spoken mantra, as I knew that we would get lost unless we were totally focused, fearless, and surrendered to this Mystery. At one point on this "road" that was no-road, we came to a waterfall that we had to go through. Now the road was completely washed away. "No fear!" I kept repeating.

After driving on in no-time, I noted a bridge over a large body of water far below. I followed its span as if I were actually driving on it; in "reality" we were still in the clouds. As the bridge met the shore, we now were on land, and I sensed that I was to turn right and park. I was now alone and felt as if I were to wait for my next Assignment, whatever that might mean."

I then awoke. It is difficult to relate the impact that this dream had on me as I saw it expressed in my writing. I felt that Wisdom was in the institute of learning and was offering Her immeasurable knowledge as gift as I wrote the first few meditations. Then, Sophia began peeking in to the meditations more and more as ballast and balance. I chose to use the name Wisdom throughout the original nineteen meditations for clarity; I added, however, a twentieth meditation to honor Sophia's harmonizing energy. They are balanced as I *experience* their unique energies. Wisdom orders all with love: humanity's heavy burdens, our sufferings, yearnings, separation, and death, for example, while Sophia encourages us to live life fully: to walk in beauty, to be mindful of Nature and Her wondrous gifts. Together, they interact in partnership with the Creator and Creation like a tapestry woven with Love.

It is my hope that as you read and ponder each meditation that you, too, may enjoy, learn from, and follow their guidance. They will lead you to the Dance, where joy, laughter, and the lightness-of-being hold sway. You may even find yourself letting go of old patterns of the past and risking steps that lead to discovering the Wellness-One- Being of Wisdom/Sophia and the Beloved at home in your heart. I'd like to share just one more synchronicity with you as you begin to read *Walking with Wisdom*. I started to write this book, quite unintentionally, while on retreat at Emery House in Massachusetts. I had just purchased a new Bible that contained the Apocrypha and began by reading Solomon's Book of Wisdom. As I usually do when studying the Bible, I began to "make it mine" by writing more contemporary lines and phrases for my own understanding and, eventually, I simply followed my own intuition and inspiration. Just as the dream seemed a blessing from Wisdom as I completed the book, so on the first morning at Emery House, Sophia gifted me in Her mischievous way, when I met a fox, who hurried away. Then, each morning of the retreat, I was greeted by some new sighting of fox. So, before returning home, I wrote a poem to honor this gift of Sophia and fox, whose energy just "happens" to be of invisibility and wisdom:

> *You eluded me*
> > *as you scurried*
> > *your red-tail flurried*
> > *in your hurried*
> > > *need to hide.*
>
> *You intrigued me*
> > *with vanishing tail*
> > *round hill and dale*
> > *you never failed*
> > > *each time to hide.*
>
> *Today you graced me*
> > *with red fox greeting*
> > *a gentle meeting*
> > *no fearful fleeting*
> > > *or need to hide.*
>
> *Did you want to see*
> > *if I would flee*
> > *perhaps, to tame me*
> > *or just to agree*
> > > *to walk as friends*
> > > > *side-by-side?*

In writing *Walking with Wisdom,* I have learned much from Wisdom and Sophia during the ten years that I have been walking with them. I pray that all who read this book will find new ways of being with Wisdom and Her guidance and teachings and with Sophia, who will brighten and lighten your lives.

So be it.

Cultivating Wisdom is a sacred Work.

Seek Her in the Silence

Within your heart.

Meditation One

Love justice, O rulers of nations,
O people of Earth!
Honor the Most High in
word and deed;
seek Wisdom of the Heart.
For Love draws nigh to those who
resist worldly temptations,
and manifests to those who live
according to spiritual laws.
Ignorance and fear fall by the wayside,
exposed
as their folly is laid bare.
Wisdom enters not a deceitful heart,
nor dwells in the house of illusion.
A holy and disciplined mind turns
from ignorance and falsehood,
ignoring their myriad distractions,

while the soul stands firm, allowing

Wisdom to have Her way.

Wisdom is a kindly spirit, yet life

holds you accountable for

all your thoughts and words;

Love is witness to your inmost feelings,

an observer of your heart,

aware of all you think and utter.

Love Consciousness fills the universe

and embraces all things, so that

nothing within can be hidden.

You who live in fear and illusion,

and spew forth false words

that cause another to suffer

will not escape notice.

You will reap the bitter fruit

of all you have sown.

A record of each thought, word, and deed

is imprinted in the Unseen Realm,

where your life is reviewed according

to the Law of Love;

this review becomes the legacy

of your earthly life.

Beware then, be mindful and walk with
wisdom, justice, and integrity,
that your soul may live in peace.

Do not separate yourself from Wisdom,
following worldly glamour;
this brings but a life of illusion
and loneliness.

Remember, each life is a gift of Love:
Wisdom and the Beloved delight in unity—
not in the destruction of life.

All things are created that
they might have being and meaning;
the generative forces of the universe
are wholesome;
they empower and give life with
no destruction in them.

Neutral and free, they are
like seeds blown on the
wings of wind that gestate and
grow into full fruition.

Justice is a quality of eternal life.

Be not like those who by their
words and deeds live separated

from Love and Light;

they live with fear and guilt,

feeling they are unworthy of love.

Unaware of true justice,

they do not feel close

to the Beloved,

Who, with Wisdom,

ever awaits them.

Pleasure eventually leads to sorrow.

Wisdom leads the soul to lasting joy.

Awaken! Experience Sophia's delight!

Meditation Two

The unawakened rationalize their words
and deeds, saying to themselves,
"Our lives are but a fleeting shadow
filled with pain and sorrow,
and we all die in the end.
Were we not born by chance
with no remembrance of our living?
Is our breath naught but smoke,
and reason simply
a spark enkindled
by the beating of our hearts?
Will not the body
return to ashes,
and the spirit disappear into
the atmosphere?
Even our name will be forgotten in time.
Who will recall our deeds?

Our life will fade like the traces

of a cloud and be scattered

like mist chased by the rays of the sun,

consumed by its heat.

Our allotted time is like the passing

of the seasons.

There is no return from our dying

because death is sealed; thus, no one

can avoid it or turn back."

Truly, they are misled;

their hearts and minds are

not aware of their innate potential

and purpose. *So* thinking only

of themselves, they do not notice

true Life passing them by, and

they plod along, missing the joy

and delight of Wisdom's guiding spirit.

Unawakened to Love and Wisdom,

they project their inner wounds

out to others and cry:

"Come, let us enjoy what we will, and

take from creation all that we desire.

Let us fill ourselves with the best wine

and purchase all we can to enhance

our beauty and stature,

letting no thing pass us by.

Let no place we go be free from

our revelry; let us

leave signs of our pleasures

wherever we may be.

This we must deserve;

this is our destiny.

If we oppress the needy, as well as

the just of the world,

or take advantage of the lonely

and those who are frail,

and never give heed to the sick

and the old,

what will it matter?

Who will care?

Strength and power will be how

we gain justice for ourselves.

Does not weakness prove itself useless?"

The unawakened in their ignorance

continue:

"Let us attack those who are just;

they set themselves above us

and oppose our actions;

they reproach us if we break

their laws, and

accuse us of not living up to

our birthright.

They claim to have understanding of

the Most High and

count themselves as children of Love

and friends of the Beloved.

They become for us a reproach of

our thoughts and deeds;

even to see them is distasteful,

because their lives are different

from ours, and

their ways are so strange.

They consider us debased; they treat us

as parasites on society to be taught

the ways of Love.

They declare that they are blessed

even in death, and boast

that God is their parent.

Let us test if their words are true;

let us see what happens at

the close of their lives.

If the just are the children of Love,

wouldn't the Holy One defend them,

and deliver them from the hands

of their adversaries?

Therefore, let us put them to the test

through insult and suffering,

that we may have proof of

their gentleness and faith,

and put their forbearance on trial.

Let us condemn them to shame

and to death, for

they believe that they will be protected."

Thus did those filled with fear

and illusion reason, but

they were led astray;

not knowing Wisdom and

Love's presence,

they made friends with apathy and doubt.

They knew not the hidden purposes

of the Beloved, nor

did they seek the blessings

of holiness, nor

could they discern the peace and joy

of innocent souls.

Were we not all created

with eternal life and

made in the image and nature

of the Great Birther?

Yet through ignorance and fear

of the unknown Realm of Love,

death seemed final on earth.

How can those who choose to live

in darkness come to experience

Wisdom's joy and delight, and

the Light and Peace of Love?

Sophia is ever at play.
Greet Her daily in nature, creative work
A child's imagination.
Discover the sacred in all you do.

Meditation Three

The souls of the Awakened, however,

live in Love and Light, knowing

that they can never be separated from

the Indwelling Divine Guest.

In the eyes of the ignorant

they may seem to have died,

their passing thought to be the end,

a disaster of utter destruction;

yet they are at peace.

Even if others believed

they were totally destroyed,

their hope is realized in eternal life.

Having lived their lives fully,

extending mercy and justice,

they know the Peace of Love.

They have been tested in the Fire

that refines and have not

been found wanting.

In the time of the Divine Visitation,
they will shine forth, radiating
sparks of Light out to the world.
They will guide the nations in building
community with all peoples, they will
teach the joy of sharing and
the wisdom and efficacy of
right action.
Those who follow the path of Love
will come to live with Wisdom,
and the faithful will not be bound
by fear and doubt.
For the awakened ones abound in
grace and mercy, knowing
the Great Ones watch over them.

Those who still sleep,
who walk in darkness, though,
separate themselves from Love by
their destructive words and deeds.
Oppressing others and spreading seeds of
misery and propaganda,
they disregard the tenets of Love.

Those who look not to Wisdom and
an understanding of Her ways
live in illusion;
vain are their hopes and fruitless
are their labors.
They set a misguided example to
family and friends alike, and
leave a legacy of misery and ignorance
to their children.
Blessed are those who know true Love,
who enter into union with
tenderness and commitment;
the fruits of their union will radiate
joy and delight to others.
Blessed are those whose hands and heart
have maintained justice,
who have lived in accordance with
the laws of Love;
those faithful to Love Consciousness
will hear the good counsel, the
guidance of Wisdom in their hearts.
The fruits of integrity, justice,
sharing, and compassion
bear only blessings.

Rooted in Holy Wisdom, they

will find peace and joy in their work:

for Wisdom is ever at play—

with Her, gentle guidance, work,

prayer, and play become one;

satisfaction and fulfillment

are their own reward.

Think carefully then of how you will

conduct your lives and what

you will teach future generations.

Whose lives will be remembered

with respect and honor?

Whose countenance will shine

wearing a face of wisdom

in their old age?

The one who dies—young or old—

will be welcomed Home and weighed

according to the harvest of his or her life.

How generously did you share?

To whom did you extend Love?

Glorious will be the future Life of

all keepers of the Promise.

Wisdom: a seed planted by Love
That buds and blossoms in your true Being:
Love without end.

Meditation Four

How life-giving when
we give birth to virtue;
for virtue recalls our immortality
our goodness, and our Oneness;
thus it is known by Holy Wisdom
and by humankind.
Whenever virtue is present, others
will learn of its ways, and
they will yearn for it when
it is missing;
through all generations virtue lives on,
given honor when extended with wisdom.

Yet many are those who disdain
the presence of Love, who create
their own rules;
all that they do will fade away;
their roots will be shallow,

never taking a firm hold.

Even when they do bring forth fruit
for a time, planted among
stones of ignorance, they are not sturdy;
they will be shaken by strong winds
that uproot them.

Or the branches will break and
not reach maturity; and
even if the trees do bear fruit,
they will be bitter and unfit for eating.

So it is with unholy men and women,
those who choose the ways
of ego-illusion and separation;
regrettably, they teach their children
to be people of the lie.

Yet those whose paths are just,
who live in peace and with compassion,
even if their lives are cut short,
they will leave a legacy of Love.

For age is not honored by length of years
or measured by time.

Old age and gray hair
do not confirm wisdom.

Wisdom comes to the just,
to those whose lives reflect
virtue and holiness.

Those who love Wisdom's ways open
their hearts to welcome Her, and
bid the Divine Guest enter;
they are protected when dark forces
try to seduce them; they stand firm.
They uphold the covenant of Life.
Guile does not deceive their souls.
Early death of the loving and just
may fulfill their lives,
while many years of a life unlived
may yield only empty promises.
Even so, myriad are those who see
and do not understand;
they remain deaf and blind
to eternal life.
Yes, grace and mercy dwell
with the just, and the
Holy One is no stranger to them.

May those who die for justice's sake
give witness to those bound by
fear and illusion;
may those who are yet young
follow the ways of the just,

that they might be at peace

in their elder years.

Some will listen to Wisdom's voice

and learn the virtue of Truth,

remaining steadfast under

the banner of Love.

They will know their Purpose

and keep company with all

that is life-giving.

The unjust, when they see this,

may taunt them with contempt,

all the while separating themselves

from the hope of their birthright.

Sadly, their lives will be diminished;

they may forgotten

or dishonored knowing

only the ways of ignorance.

As they face their legacy of ego-illusion

and review their unworthy words,

their fear-filled deeds,

they may recognize the truth

of their unlived potential,

the waste and misguided use

of the gift of life.

Not having known or prayed for
forgiveness, the healing balm of Love,
they will suffer anguish and regret.

They may wish they had never been born,
even as they await the reckoning
of true Justice,
not having realized that their true
being is Love without end.

Awaken Wisdom within and let it flow
Out to the world like a gardener
Sowing seeds of Life.

Meditation Five

Those who live with integrity

will be seen as witnesses to

the skeptics and demeanors

who scorned Wisdom and Truth.

Once they *see* their own darkness,

they will tremble with remorse and be

astounded by unexpected understanding;

they may begin to Awaken:

"*Are* these not the very ones whom

we derided with laughter,

those we held in utter contempt?

What fools we were!

We ridiculed their lives as crazy

and dishonored their deaths.

See how they are beloved as friends

of the Blessed One,

how they are numbered

among the saints.
We who have strayed far from truth,
the light of justice does not
shine on us;
clouds of deceit obscure the sun
of righteousness for us.
We, who filled our days with
lies and violence,
traveled in a barren desert
of loneliness and separation;
at the ways of Love we sneered.
And what did our arrogance avail us?
What have our ill-gotten gains
and boasting afforded us?"

"They all passed
like a shadow,
like a fleeting moment;
like ships in a stormy sea, which
when they pass leave no trail,
no pathway in the waves;
or like a caravan caught in
a desert windstorm, stung
by biting, blistering sand pellets.

They thirst for the pure,
clean water of life, while
the winds erase any trace
of their journey as if
they had never been;
they are like once-flowing rivers
turned to sludge from
pollution wrought by greed that
secretly poisons Earth
and Her creatures.
So we, born children of the Creator,
turned from Love and became
blinded to truth and justice,
lured by fear's desire for control."

Yes, those who live ignorant of
Love and Wisdom's ways
are like the fluff of dandelions
borne away by the wind
or like mist in the sunlight;
like smoke scattered by wind currents
or like lost memories
from childhood.

However, those who live in harmony

with the Divine Plan are led

to fertile fields to work as

gardeners on the Beloved's land.

They receive the gifts and blessings

of Wisdom's abundant store, and

they shine like beautiful jewels,

sharing everything in equal measure;

sheltered in the Heart of Love, they

abide in peace beyond measure.

They wear the armor of truth and

are quick to respond with equity

to those in need;

they teach and model justice

throughout their lives.

They don peace as a breastplate

and spread goodwill like

a farmer sowing seeds;

they take love as an invincible shield

and integrity as a mighty sword,

while the universe supports

their labors of Love.

They unite knowledge and wisdom

to instruct the ignorant;

clouds of fear and doubt

melt away and, like well-aimed

arrows, they find their mark.

Their energy of compassion and mercy

enter flawlessly

into every open heart

like lightning piercing the darkness.

Wisdom will make Herself known

like a mighty wind

winnowing out all

that would lay waste to Earth;

She will evoke new understandings

in all receptive hearts.

Silence is like a fence around Wisdom

Surrounding and quieting the mind.

Listen in the Silence with open heart.

Meditation Six

Awaken! Awaken to Wisdom's counsel,

all people on earth, so that

together, we may create the values

and conditions in which we

choose to live.

Listen, all who wield power

over the nations: heed

the real needs of the people;

let Wisdom be your guide.

Remember! True authority belongs

to the Creator of Earth, our home.

Here the Beloved and Wisdom

probe our hearts and minds

and scrutinize our decisions,

questioning:

"Who among you as servants

of the Most High

live with insight and compassion,

ever mindful of the Divine Plan,

aspiring to be co-creators with Love?

How will you be weighed on

the scales of justice, aware

that to whom much is given,

much more will be exacted?"

The humble, free from illusion and pride,

have learned the freedom of forgiveness,

while those who usurp their power

remain enslaved by fear and its

unsavory companions.

Wisdom is impartial to all,

great or small; She favors

not one over another,

caring for all alike; yet,

a rigorous searching of hearts awaits

the mighty, all those who wield power.

To you, therefore, O leaders in

seats of authority, are

these words addressed, that

you may aspire to know Wisdom, to

remain attuned to the Divine Guest

indwelling in every receptive heart.

To those who reverence and follow the

divine Laws of love, justice, and mercy,

you will be counted as holy;

you will be numbered among

the friends of the Friend.

Therefore, desire first to follow

the Divine Will and

heed the voice of Wisdom;

you will be heard and instructed.

Resplendent and eternal is Wisdom,

readily perceived by those who listen

in the Silence of the heart.

Wisdom hastens to make Herself known;

She is available to all who

love and seek Her;

one who awakens Her from within

will not be disappointed;

for Wisdom awaits at the threshold.

Honoring Her through mindfulness

leads to peace and understanding,

and those who remain vigilant for Her sake

will reap blessings to share with others;

for Wisdom makes Her own rounds,

seeking those ready to listen;
She graciously awakens them in ways
known only to the heart,
greeting them with attentive care.

Harken! Her ways are filled with
joy, mindfulness, and mystery.
She easily evokes smiles as
She opens our hearts' eyes to
the breadth, beauty, and wonder
of Nature's blessed gifts;
She is ever a healing balm
to the soul.

The first step toward meeting Wisdom
is an earnest desire for Her;
to love Her is to honor Her laws;
to observe Her laws is
the root of righteousness
and the basis for impeccability.
Being pure in heart brings one
close to the Beloved;
thus, to heed Wisdom's counsel
leads to living in the Realm of Love.

If then you find fulfillment in
authority and leadership, become
a servant of and for the people;
honor Wisdom, that you may
serve in peace and joy with
the true Friend of your heart!
Now what Wisdom is and how She
came to be, I shall reveal,
withholding no secrets from you;
for your own knowledge,
I shall search out and
bring to light Her mysteries,
holding only to the truth.
Neither shall I permit fear or pride
to enter in, because
fear and ego-illusions cannot
keep company with Wisdom.
Needed in the world are multitudes
who love Wisdom and stand ready
to serve in healing and protecting
the planet;
prudent leaders of integrity can bring
peace and stability to the people.

So heed these life-giving teachings

which lead to well-being,

that you may be a blessing to all whom

you meet and serve along the way.

Wisdom teaches all who listen
With spiritual ears.
Children, in their spontaneous play,
Already have met Sophia.
We can learn from them.

Meditation Seven

I am mortal, the same as all others,
a descendant of everyone who
came before me—even from the first.
In my mother's womb I developed into
a human being over nine months—
body, mind, heart, and soul—
from a union of seed and egg
in the joy of marriage.
And when I was born, I inhaled
the common air, as a new
community member of precious Earth;
wailing, I uttered that first sound
that we all made.
In simple clothing and with constant care,
I was nurtured.
*N*o child of the Eternal Begetter has
any different origin or birth;

for the entry into life is similar for all,
and by the same Doorway, do we exit life.

In my youth as I learned to pray
with a receptive and sincere heart,
I received understanding;
I called on the Most High, and
the spirit of Wisdom came upon me
that I might share it with others;
so as we persist in prayer, ever
listening for words of guidance, one day—
whether in a sudden moment of grace,
or after a lifetime of expectation—
the spirit of Wisdom makes Herself known.

Ever after we will prefer Wisdom
above all else, for
nothing is as precious as She is;
in Her presence, gold is as sand
and silver is as mud.

Beyond power and riches, food and drink,
is Her splendor, that never yields
to the darkness.

In Her company, all good things
are brought together;
as we remain in Her company,
blessings multiply.

Rejoice in them all, for Wisdom
is their origin;
delight in the Mother of them all.
Learn of Wisdom's simplicity, and
share generously with all people;
Her riches hide not away,
for She is an unfailing treasure;
those who gain this treasure are
friends of the Beloved; so
garner the gifts that Wisdom teaches
with Her gentle guidance.
Grant, O Beloved, that I speak with
humility and understanding,
that I honor Wisdom's endowments
as sacred, beyond measure.
For You are Her companion and
You correct even the wise.
Our thoughts and words are
in Your hands;
You are the director of all our actions.
You help us to discern our own gifts
so we may share them with others.
You give us knowledge of
all existing things that
we may know our interdependence

with the whole universe and
the power of all its elements:
the **chronos** and **kairos** of time,
of living in the present moment,
the Eternal Now;
the positions of the stars and planets,
the variation of the seasons,
the cycles of millennia, the natures of
our sisters and brothers,
animal, fish, and fowl;
the power of spirits, the thoughts
of humankind,
the uses of plant life, their gifts of
beauty, food, and healing,
as well as the air we breathe.
All of creation is given that
we might learn to share
its bounty as sacred gift;
and Wisdom, who discerns the inner
quality and relationship of all things,
will teach everyone who listens
with inner spiritual ears.
For within Wisdom is a spirit that is pure,
intelligent, sacred, unique, diverse,
subtle, active, clear, assured,

in no way harmful, loving what is good,

beneficent, and free.

She is steadfast, reliable, serene,

all-powerful, overseeing all,

embracing all spirits—

those who are most knowledgeable,

and even those spirits most veiled.

Wisdom is more mobile than

any motion, She penetrates and

pervades all things.

She stands as an emanation,

a luminous radiation beside

the glory of the Holy One,

as a pure expression of creative power;

therefore, nothing impure can ever

penetrate Her.

For She is a resplendence of

the eternal Light, a spotless mirror

reflecting the ever-active eternal Power,

an image of Divine Love's goodness.

Wisdom, by Herself, can do all things.

She renews all things as

She herself endures;

and entering into holy souls

from generation to generation,

She Awakens them so that they become

friends of the Beloved and

prophets who are divinely inspired.

The Beloved of all hearts loves all

who dwell with Wisdom.

Who but Wisdom is fairer

than the sun, and surpasses

every constellation

of the stars?

Even in the light, She takes precedence;

there is no darkness of the night,

nor shadows of evil or ignorance

that can prevail over Wisdom.

To know Wisdom is to feel

Her presence in all things:

Nature is Her special venue.

You may see Her one misty morn

as a dozen or more tiny finches

alight on branches

just outside your window,

or feel Her in the breezes

of a blue, puffy clouded sky

as you sail in full wind

over ocean waves; though

you may be unaware of Her

guiding aid if danger calls, yet

Her hands are ever there

to lift you up.

Wisdom may shine you a blessing

through the eyes of a humble stranger

sitting with begging bowl,

even as you pass by unaware.

She heeds not the station of

anybody, but has insight into

everyone through

the Oneness of all Being;

She knows that our lives

are ephemeral, that what matters

is not the number of our days,

but the quality of how

we live each one of them.

Wisdom recognizes us each time

we are born into a new life;

She welcomes our return and continues

to guide us to new beginnings,

to other rounds in the spiral

of our sojourns toward

enlightenment.

Wisdom is even present to the

terrible waste and misery

of war and all manner of violence,
where many a heart is broken,
many a life lost before
reaching its potential.
To comfort a broken spirit,
She may inspire that soul to
choose life and embark on
a new path that offers
surprises of blessing and joy.
For Wisdom knows every heart
and loves every soul.
To cut through the heaviness
of this dark age,
She must strengthen the wills
of the hordes addicted to
inane worldly messages
that deaden the mind
and harden the heart.
Wisdom works Her ways
with mercy and kindness,
ever mindful that our wills
are free; She knows that
one day, all our childish choices
may give cause for regret.
She is not officious, nor

would She nag, control, or scold!
No! Her ways lead to Oneness,
like a dancer who becomes
the dance, or
like one who prays and becomes
the prayer; or
like a fiddler who plays with
such fervor and fun that
even the most reticent
at the gathering will engage
themselves unaware, beating to
the rhythm of the Dance.
Wisdom's way is of invitation:
She invites one and all
to join Her in celebration,
to dance with Her into
the fullness and fearlessness
of a good time, a good life.

Wisdom extends to all ends
Of the universe.
Embracing all, She has no limits.
She is found among the simple and profound
alike.

Meditation Eight

Indeed Wisdom extends to all
ends of the universe,
and She governs with benevolence
for the good of all.
Seek Her always from youth to
your elder years;
open your heart to Her
and learn Her precepts.
She brings nobility to humanity.
Her beauty reflects companionship
with the Beloved.
Great is Her knowledge of the Divine
and She will instruct you
in the Work of Love.
If riches are what you desire,
what is a greater treasure
than Wisdom,

who is at the heart of all things?
And if understanding renders service,
who in the world is more effective
than Wisdom,
who is the activator of all things?
For all who love and honor justice,
the fruits of Her works are virtues;
She teaches moderation and
common sense,
justice, integrity, and fortitude;
what is more useful than these?
If one yearns for deep understanding,
Wisdom recalls the past
and foresees the future.
She understands the turn of an adage,
the solution to riddles;
of signs and wonders She is forewarned,
and knows the unfolding
of the seasons and times.

Learn to invite Wisdom
into your life; know that
She will offer good counsel,
comfort, and encouragement

in times of care and sorrow.

But, when we call upon Wisdom

for our own acclaim,

we lose honor among the elders;

we act out of childish ego and illusion.

When we seek power and glamour,

Wisdom cuts through our arrogance

like a flaming sword, even as

She reflects the reality of Love.

She knows the efficacy of silence

and encourages us to embrace it;

then our words will be attended, and

our peace extend out

to the world.

By honoring Wisdom's words, listening

for Her guidance in the silence,

we will act in accordance with Love

and leave a worthy legacy for

generations to come.

As more and more people become

wise through Her counsel,

the nations will share

and live in peace.

Wars will cease as resources are

fairly distributed; and
there will be plenty for all.
At home in the evening, we can find
rest with Her;
for Wisdom is an ever-present
companioning Presence;
when we attune to Her Voice,
peace and gladness abide
in our hearts.

These are good thoughts and
deep reflections for the heart;
for by kinship with Wisdom, our fears
will diminish, our love capacity grow.
In friendship with Wisdom comes insight;
working in harmony with Her, we find
satisfaction and fulfillment;
by following Her ways, we serve
the Divine Plan for Earth.
Creation is a Divine Gift;
we share in this Gift inasmuch as
we honor our birthright.
Knowing that we cannot possess Wisdom,
that She, too, is pure Gift,

we can with gratitude welcome

Her presence within us, and aspire

to walk in Her ways with intent,

integrity, and commitment.

And with our whole heart, we can pray.

Knowledge and understanding of all things
Belong to Wisdom, Who hastens
To make Herself known to all
Who seek and desire Her.

Meditation Nine

O Blessed One of all ages,
Merciful Counselor, through
Love and Wisdom
You formed humankind
to live harmoniously with all
the creatures You fashioned,
to reverence and to care for Creation
as a sacred trust,
living kindly and justly with
integrity and a holy purpose.
Grant us the wisdom to co-create;
reject us not from among
your friends.
For we are your willing servants
through common birth,
weak and mortal, yet gaining
in strength and understanding

as we follow Wisdom's way; for

even one without blemish

is viewed as incomplete without

the wisdom that flows from You.

You have trusted us to serve in

the Divine Plan, to extend peace,

share with others, and live justly.

Love fashioned each one of us

as a holy temple, placing

an altar in the Chalice of our hearts,

even as the Crystal City on

the holy mountain of old.

With You is Wisdom, She who gives

understanding to your works;

She co-created the entire world

with You;

deep is Her knowledge of

the nuances of Divine Law

and all that is honorable.

Send Her forth from the holy mountain,

and from the Realm of Love

dispatch Her, that we may know

Her presence with us as we do your work,

as we learn how best to serve.

Knowledge and understanding of

all things belong to Wisdom;

let Her bring guidance and blessings

that lead us to right action, and

protect us with Her radiance.

Then we will live worthily, with justice

and clear discernment, bringing honor

to You, O loving companioning Presence.

For who alone can comprehend the

great Mystery? *Or*, who can see

into the heart of Wisdom?

Too often the reasoning of humankind

is but illusion, our decisions

are fraught with dark shadows;

the denseness of our being weighs heavily

on the lightness of our souls,

seeming to hold our hearts

and our minds in bondage.

May we take time

to bless and reverence

our holy home, Mother Earth,

to turn our labors into

the sacred service of Love.

For through Wisdom's guidance,

seeds of our hidden potential

may be quickened as

we hear and heed Her

inner promptings of Love.

Learning to listen to Wisdom

is an art form,

where, little by little,

we become attuned to our

own divine expressions of Love.

Then, blossoming from our inner

sacred space of silence,

we may discover that we have

created a heart-garden

that will bear fruit in due season.

And what is this fruit

but joy and the choice to serve

and co-create with

Love and Wisdom

as we are led.

Who among us is aware of

the Unseen Realm—

the great company of angels, saints,

the cloud of witnesses

and guides who ever-await

our readiness to serve with them?

Who has learned the blessing of silence,

listening for Wisdom's gentle whispers

that awaken the soul and evoke

intuitions of the heart?

Is this not the way our paths

are made straight, the way

we learn to let Wisdom guide us?

You, O Beloved, with Wisdom are

grace and pure blessing to

the whole world.

We are never alone.
We live embraced by the infinite
Power of Love and Wisdom,
Who provide us with strength as
We walk through the ages
Toward wholeness.

Meditation Ten

From the beginning of Earth's evolution
Wisdom has been present as
a protector of the inner life,
a continuous, constant guide
to shelter us through the darkness
while encouraging our growth.
Wisdom provides us with strength
as we walk through the ages
toward wholeness.
Throughout millennia, we have
strayed and separated ourselves
from Her with fear and ignorance;
thus, violence and rage did enter our hearts.
When the Earth mirrored human darkness,
a flood came to cleanse the land;
Wisdom was present and saved us by
steering a creature-filled ark

to safety with the help of
one righteous man.

When the people and nations had
fallen from grace through their
evil ways and misguided choices,
Wisdom recognized this man
and brought his act before
the Beloved;
She kept him strong all through
the travail, honoring the
compassion he had for his children.

Wisdom rescued him when those
separated from Love's ways
were perishing;
he escaped the inferno that
descended on five cities.
Nations beware! *Evidence*
of their evil remains as a
reminder to all generations:
poisoned lands where fruit
does not ripen,
nuclear waste deposits that serve as

a wake-up call to every soul.

Because we pass Wisdom by,

we are often hindered from seeing

what is good; all this is

a reminder of the ignorance, folly,

and dire consequence of not heeding

Wisdom's voice.

Wisdom rescues from trouble

those who serve Her

in the great Plan.

When all who are peaceful

and still, who listen in the Silence,

flee from mistaken ways,

She guides them on straight paths;

She awakens them to the Realm of Love

here on earth, and they come

to spiritual understanding;

they learn to follow their purpose

and are blessed abundantly.

When others oppress them,

they are humble, and share

their riches gladly, with equity.

She protects them from fear

as they face deceptive ways,

and keeps them safe when danger
draws nigh; in all they do,
She helps them to succeed,
so they might come to know
that heeding Wisdom's guidance
is powerful beyond measure.
For unlike those who stray from
Her ways and do not understand,
Wisdom will draw those who love Her
upward toward the infinite variety
and beauty of Love,
to the love and inner light
of their own soul and spirit.

Wisdom is ever mindful of each life.
When a righteous man was sold,
She descended with him
into the prison depths,
and did not leave until
She empowered him with
a nation, giving him
authority over unjust rulers.
Those who had accused him
She proved to be false,

and gave lasting honor

to this virtuous soul.

Wisdom delivered a holy

and beleaguered people

from a nation of oppressors.

She entered the soul

of a faithful servant,

who withstood powerful rulers

with wonders and signs.

She rewarded the sojourners

for their labors;

She guided them along

Love's way,

becoming a shelter to them

by day, a starry flame

throughout the night.

She guided them over

the Red Sea,

leading them through

deep waters, but

She allowed their enemies

to drown in the sea

of unconsciousness.

Thus, the awakened witnessed

to the unjust,

singing hymns of praise

and thanksgiving;

and with one accord they

praised Wisdom's defending hand;

She opened the mouths

of those who were mute,

and made the tongues

of the young to

speak clearly.

Wisdom knows the limitations of

living in this world of duality,

the extremes of opposites; yet

when we become fully awakened,

illuminated in Her radiance,

the Oneness of All Being

shines through.

Blessed are those to whom

She reveals Her brilliance

within every heart where

She makes Her home.

Living by the letter of the law
Can imprison and engender fear;
Living by the spirit of the Law is Wisdom,
Who helps us face our fears and
Withstand our doubts.

Meditation Eleven

Wisdom prospers our work

delighting us with joy

as we surrender ourselves

into Her guiding hand.

Even when we journey

through times

of loneliness and challenges,

even if we seem to live

in a desert of dry bones,

She helps us face our fears

and withstand our doubts.

When we thirst for new life,

we can call upon Her,

and like living water,

new life flows into

our arid and empty hearts.

Though seeming separation

arises from our fears,

Wisdom's way brings relief

and freedom.

You may find yourself drawn to

the ease of Her laughter,

laughter that can liberate

an imprisoned mind or

an unimaginative heart from

old patterns that no longer serve.

Freed from the fear of risk or change,

a doorway may open

to refresh your soul

and lighten your spirit.

Like the calming flow of

an ever-running river,

Her counsel brings an awakening

that honors the power of Love:

the stream of our own

true Being.

She shows how our thirst

for Wisdom's way

is rewarded with understanding.

Then, when we are challenged,

when we face dire circumstances
that evoke fear and doubt with
all their illusionary companions,
we learn the ways of mercy,
patience, and peace; we see
with the eyes of our heart,
unlike those who seek to
blame and condemn.

For She offers us opportunities
to learn and grow that may
test our very souls,
while Justice weighs our
every thought and action.

When we turn away from
love and kindness,
when we choose to ignore
Wisdom's promptings,
we are like spoiled children
wanting our own way.

Yet we are no longer young;
we are accountable for
the wounds we inflict.

When awakened, we come to
rue our wanton ways.

For when we scorn those
who seem different from us,
and cast them away
like unwanted trash,
in the end, we will see
ourselves, as our exaggerated
illusions of superiority are
shattered, in need of healing.

In return for our foolish
and mistaken thoughts
and titillated by
glamor, power, and money,
we draw to ourselves a
multitude of lessons that
seem like punishment,
so that we might learn from
the very wrongs we have wrought.
For the all-powerful loving Mind,
which created the world
out of formlessness,
did not lack the means
to send us many opportunities
to awaken,

whether they be wild storms

that destroy life and

Your handiwork, or whether they be

the greedy misuse of power

that destroys the planet and

creates chaos in the cosmos.

Do we not yet understand

that our negative thinking,

our unrestrained use of energy,

wreak dire effects

upon the Earth?

We are held accountable;

for our every action is

imprinted upon our soul.

The unjust of the world will

soon scatter and fall,

while those who know Wisdom

will surely reap peace and joy

as they serve with

Love and Wisdom.

So awaken from your deep slumber,

drop the false masks of ignorance

and illusion.

Climb the ladder of aspiration,

and inspiration—and soar!
Allow beauty, justice, sharing, and
freedom to pave a pathway
to a renewed civilization.
Concern yourself not with those
who seek power, profit and privilege;
they see only wealth,
not knowing the true treasure,
the pearl of great price,
dwelling within each soul.

Wisdom teaches the power
of simply Being, that in
our weakness is true strength;
yet who can understand
the efficacy of no effort?
The whole world before You
is like a speck in
the cosmos and galaxies,
like a drop of morning dew
that falls to the ground.
You, who are merciful to all,
and can do all things,
You overlook our mistakes,

as we ask for forgiveness.

You love all things that exist;

all that You have co-created

is for blessing, since

You would not have made

anything unless it was life-giving.

How would anything have

endured if You had

not willed it?

Or how would anything

not called forth by You

have been preserved?

You spare all things, for

with Wisdom,

they are yours, O Beloved,

You who, together,

love your Creation.

Wisdom grows in us season by season
And may take a lifetime;
Yet, You love us all and grant us
Free will to take our own time
To choose our own way.

Meditation Twelve

Your immortal Spirit abides

within all things as

Love Consciousness.

You correct little by little

those who miss the way,

awakening them to the illusions

through which they stray,

so they may know Your

loving companioning Presence

and trust You, O Beloved!

O Holy Wisdom!

Those who lived long ago

within Your Creation

turned from You with

their wanton, evil deeds

that destroyed the balance

with their unholy rites,

their merciless slaughter

of children, and

their sacrificial feasting

on human flesh and blood—

this was not Wisdom,

this was not Love.

So these initiates who

had chosen the dark path,

and parents who cared not

for innocent lives—

to maintain the balance—

they were destroyed,

so that a worthy settlement

of people in the service

of the Holy One

could now inhabit the land.

Today, in your mercy,

You spare those who defy You,

warning them that their

unholy ways will lead

only to their demise.

You choose not to deliver

the unholy ones into

the hands of the virtuous

in battle, or

to destroy them through

your strength with vengeance.

But by the power of Love,

even recognizing their

evil ways, You freely

offer them opportunities

to repent, aware

that their firmly held ways

may once again turn

them from your Love.

From the beginning they

have looked only to themselves,

and, in the end, condemn

themselves through their stubborn

commitment to power and control.

Who will ask,

What have You done?

or resist your judgment?

Who will accuse You

for the destruction

that ensues?

Who will come before You

to plead as an advocate

for the unjust?

For there is no one besides

Love and Wisdom whose

care is for all people;

no one to whom

You must prove that You

judge not unjustly;

nor can any authority

confront You about those

who turn from You.

You are righteous and

You rule all things rightly,

deeming it a misuse of power

to condemn others; for eventually,

the unjust fail and fall

by their own actions.

For Your strength is

the source of righteousness,

and your sovereignty over all

causes You to spare all.

You reveal your strength

when people doubt that

your Power is a blessing,
and You confront any
injustice wherever
You find it.
Although You are sovereign
in strength, You judge
with gentleness; and
with great forbearance
You guide us.
You love us all and
grant us free will
to choose our own way.

Through Love and Wisdom
all peoples can learn of
Your justice and kindness,
of how You fill your children
with a holy hope, even as You
forgive their trespasses.
When needed, You chasten them
with loving care and respect,
even those who turn from
You with disdain and disbelief,
granting them time and every

opportunity to awaken

to your Love.

With amazing grace

You bless our lives

and uphold your Promise

to be with us always.

So while we may flounder

and regress to old ways,

succumbing to power-filled desires,

You allow us our illusions

so that, as we are ready,

we are humbled and

know once again the blessings

of your ever merciful

and accepting Heart of Love.

Because You give us free will,

those who live unconsciously,

following a life of folly and fear,

will learn in the end that they must

reap all that they have sown;

for when we stray onto

paths of illusion,

accepting as gods the glitter

of power, greed, and
self-serving ways,
we deceive ourselves and
follow not our true Purpose.
Therefore, like children who
cannot yet reason, we
mock Wisdom's guidance
so freely available to all.
Those too blind
to see their foolishness
miss the peace and joy
of serving and sharing
in the Plan for Earth.
Yet as they suffer through
their meaningless desires
in all the ways that they
think to be treasure, they will
eventually become dissatisfied;
then they will see and recognize
the truth and wisdom of
the Holy One whom they had
refused to acknowledge.
Then they will weep and
yearn and turn

toward Love and Light;
in the end they will finally
become mindful of
Love and Wisdom at
the Heart of the world:
Christ Consciousness.

Wisdom teaches us the art of living
In balance and harmony;
To learn from Her in the Silence
Is to receive higher thoughts
And understanding.

Meditation Thirteen

Individuals who choose
ignorance over Love's ways
are foolish by nature;
they are blind to the beauty
and tapestry of Creation.
They know not its Source,
nor do they recognize
the Great Architect
even as they enjoy gifts
from Nature's bounty.
Rather, being asleep,
they do not understand that
fire, wind, or Earth energies
or the panoply of the stars,
or the fathoms of ocean depths,
or the luminaries of heaven
live in us as symbols.

For sacred natural phenomena

are hidden in things;

Wisdom finds them and

reveals them to us

as we learn to see

with our inner eyes of Love.

These amazing elements

of Creation, people

thought them to be gods;

yet, as they awakened,

they soon discovered

how much more than

natural phenomenon

are Love and Wisdom in

the unity of diversity:

Oneness.

The people were overwhelmed

at the power and patterns

of this universal display, but how

much more wondrous than these

is the One who formed them?

For from the majesty and beauty

of created things comes

a corresponding perception
of their Creator.
Even when the people err
in their understanding,
Wisdom condemns them not
in their searching for Love.
For as they live in
creation's abundance, their
heart's desire urges them on;
they learn to trust in the
splendors they see—
and all of it is beautiful.
Yet, often their experience
remains limited, their
inner light dim.
For, if they remain ignorant
of Love's power and authority,
how will they discover
the secret, hidden home
of Wisdom:
the human heart?

All is not lost, however.
To open your heart

is to receive higher

thoughts and understanding;

yet, be aware!

Know that fear lurks

in the shadows,

ever ready to lure

seekers from the path.

Don the armor of courage.

Light radiates like sunshine

in peace and harmony,

while tremors of dark

tumultuous storms cloud

hearts, minds, and souls

wherever fear abides.

Sift negativity from your thoughts,

all that are not life-giving.

Truth and kindness

go a long way

in awakening those whose

hearts remain closed,

asleep and too deaf to hear.

To all who have awakened:

answer the Call;

partner with the Holy Ones:

become Teachers of Love.

Few know that the way

is prepared for everyone;

heed Wisdom's Voice:

the inward journey to

your own true Self.

Listen not to those

whose lives witness not

to kindness and justice;

truth resides in the Silence

where the Word

can be heard.

Though myriad roads await

the seeker, follow

your own way to Love,

enlightened by Guidance;

know that you are never alone.

Even the unjust find

healing and solace in Love;

through forgiveness

all is clothed in holiness.

Be on guard.

Call upon Wisdom's counsel

to guide and protect you

from missteps along the way;

for fear is ever close by,

ready to undermine with

all its many distractions.

Wisdom flows from the Center
Of Divine Light into the inner Chapel
Of our receptive hearts;
Allow the springs of Life from
The unseen Source to flow
In and through you.

Meditation Fourteen

Do not place your trust

in passing trends, nor

in promises made

by manipulators of words.

False idols of wealth, fame

and military might

are like a game of chess,

where the poor become pawns

of those whose purses are filled

to overflowing.

Rather, like one preparing

to sail across the ocean,

have faith in

the Beloved of all hearts

knowing that Divine Providence

will help you steer

the Course; and that

through Wisdom's good counsel

a safe passage will

keep you from peril

so that you reach

the Distant Shore

in safety.

There your soul is

at peace, humbled

by the new Life

beyond the Veil as

you reach the pinnacle

of joy:

Oneness with All.

Blessed are those who have

planted seeds of peace

for the generations to come.

Awakening to your inter-being

with all souls, you

experience that you are

One in being with love,

forever linked and inspired

by Creation Itself.

Thus, in awakening, you are

blessed beyond riches;

for as you extend peace,

love, and light to others,

it returns to you in full measure.

Therefore, the wise know that

worldly glory is tenuous,

and any material success

but a fleeting pleasure; for

all the world's riches and power

are rendered useless

by death.

Put aside yesterday's

thoughts and habits;

let go of former misdeeds,

and with true remorse

forgive yourself and others

the consequences of hurtful

unholy thoughts and deeds.

Call upon Love and Wisdom

to lead you from vanities

and all temptation to repeat

past patterns.

Allow the springs of Life
to flow in and through you
from the unseen Source,
Divine Light,
which awakens life-giving energy
to flow freely through your
inmost Centers and to
maintain your life-balance.
Imagine this sacred Source
of your being, of All being,
entering each soul,
imparting Love and Light
to awaken the soul's
full potential.
How you respond to this
Life-Force, this gift
of Living-Light,
depends on your will.
Will the choices you make
flower from inspiration
and give birth to
new ideas and creative
ways of sharing?

Or, will you scoff at Love,

unaware of your true nature,

and choose to follow worldly

patterns of illusive pleasures

that limit freedom and

spawn addictions?

By cultivating communication with

Wisdom's inner guidance

through prayer and meditation

in the Silence,

your suffering diminishes;

you are no longer a slave to

fear and negative forces; you

become a co-creator with Wisdom

and Cosmic Intelligence.

Yet, how much longer will

ignorance foster

nightmares of fear that

waste energy and stifle

the blossoming of one's true Self?

When will we learn to live

by the Universal Laws that

govern Truth and supersede

worldly law?

Providing guidelines to life
for everyone, these
Laws bring justice to all.
Why focus on a world that
has gone awry, when
following the Law of Love
brings order and assurance,
lifting our souls to
heightened and keen knowing?

Aware or unaware, everyone
lives in many dimensions.
We are inexorably interconnected.
What we do or think
affects others as well as
the very Cosmos Itself.
When consciously committed
to living within these Laws,
we manifest goodness
and extend Love.
To realize that we create
our own reality through
the energy of our

every thought, word, deed,

and feeling may shake us awake.

For we have only the now-moment.

The past is over, give it no power.

The future is uncertain, it fosters anxiety.

Our truth is here in the eternal now.

Dark forces ever await entry

into your life.

Protect yourself!

Hold fast to the Light

and give them not your energy

or power to weaken your spirit,

to deaden your soul.

Discipline your mind

to reject negative thoughts

that can lead to depression.

Envision your life filled with

Light, peace, and harmony.

Let your transformation

extend out to the world

that the Laws of Love may reign.

Wisdom with Love will one day
Melt the frozen hearts of those
Who remain closed to their potential.
Love will grow in us as we push
The edges of our own will and
Choose to embrace the Silence.

Meditation Fifteen

The precepts of Love and Wisdom

are just and true;

listen for Wisdom's gentle Voice

to guide and inspire you.

Even when you miss the mark,

closing your heart's ears,

afraid to change and grow,

She patiently awaits your

readiness to Awaken.

So it behooves us to listen,

to trust the process,

the mystery of our

journey home to Love.

Aspire, then, to Love,

reach toward it

to your highest potential,

and align your Self

with the Divine Order.

When the Light within

grows brighter, and

the Love within expands,

goodness, even miracles,

will seem natural.

You will come to know

the beauty and power

of diversity in

the Oneness of all life.

Yet, myriad are those

who prefer the status quo,

who are afraid to risk,

who choose comfort

and apathy over the

challenges of right action,

which lead to fulfillment,

assurance, and all the blessings

that give birth to joy.

All through their lives, those

who have yet to awaken,

yearn for Something more, yet

they turn to material things

and banal distractions,

hoping to be fulfilled and satisfied.

Some turn to spirits,

drugs, and other addictions,

anything to numb the feelings

of inner despair and boredom.

For they know not Wisdom,

Her understanding ways

and clear counsel.

Unaware of Her closeness,

Her desire to lead them

to Love and Light to discover

each one's unique, yet hidden gifts,

fear companions them through

all their dreams and desires.

They are satisfied with crumbs

while a banquet awaits them.

Their days are dreary, their

nights restless with discontent.

Regrettably, they are ignorant

of their plight; for

they have become deaf to

the inner promptings

of Wisdom's Voice.

Believing that they are merely
physical beings, they do not
understand the meaning of
the spiritual experiences that
sometimes surprise them:
they tend to rationalize and dismiss
them as simply imagination.
In due season, however,
they will come to realize
that, in truth, they have
ever been spiritual beings
having physical experiences.

The unawakened desire love
not knowing of the
One true Love, Who
accompanies all who
open their hearts and souls
to bid the Divine Guest enter.
Still, Wisdom and Love will
one day, whether in this life
or in the Life to come,
melt their frozen hearts.

Webs woven in the midst
of confused, negative thoughts
may pierce a sensitive heart
like a poison arrow;
they deaden the spirit.
These thoughtforms linger unseen
and sully the atmosphere,
seeking like parasites
an unsuspecting host.
Powerful are fear-based thoughts!
Ego-driven, they are illusions
that sow seeds of doubt
into hearts and minds
too busy to listen within.
If these seed-thoughts
are allowed to grow,
they can have a gradual
and cumulative effect that
seem to diminish the soul's
natural expression:
freedom, truth, justice,
peace, gratitude, and Love.
They poison and separate the
heart from freedom, integrity,

responsibility, and purpose.
Beware! Call upon Wisdom for
counsel and guidance;
gird yourself with forgiveness,
assurance, right thoughts,
Love, and Light.
The darkness will then diminish.
With Wisdom within your heart,
all mistaken thoughts, those
that reflect fear, doubt,
or guilt and seem to
separate you from expressing
the love and joy you are,
the Potential you bear,
can be corrected by
changing your thoughts.
Mindfulness, moment by moment,
is like a filter for your thoughts;
hence, clarity of mind becomes
a blessing in praise of Wisdom.
Right thoughts lead to
right relationship and action.

Each moment is precious.
Take time in stillness to listen
To the heart's counsel.
Wisdom abides there.

Meditation Sixteen

Beams of Light pierce
through the wilderness of
ego-desires that seem
to separate and divide—
illusions that mean nothing.
Only One Love and One Mind
are real. *Wisdom* ever awaits
our response, our yes, to
Her invitation to guide us Home
to the Realm of Love,
which is ever available in
this life or in
Life beyond the Veil.
Our souls will sing and
rejoice as the lure
of shadow-pleasures fades,
giving way to simplicity and silence,

stillness and solitude,

where Wisdom makes Her home.

Gladly, She leads us to Service,

to a Work of Love that reflects

our unique gifts, which we

can, now, joyfully choose

to express in the Plan for Earth,

a life that riches cannot buy:

vitality freed from fear.

Holy are cleansed hearts

open and ready to teach

the power of love and understanding

in acts of selfless service.

Purified by Love and free from all

that is spawned by misleading ways

no longer able to exert power,

the inner Heart Chapel

can radiate dazzling Light

into the darkness,

blessing all who see true.

Nothing can obstruct a heart

which is pure and which,

through spiritual eyes,

sees color prisms that

resonate clear vibrations

in harmony with the heavenly

community at peace in

the invisible realm of Love!

Here Wisdom awaits, hidden,

at one with the Mystery.

Bound by a single, silver thread

and acting in accordance with

the Higher Will,

teachings of true Life manifest

loving ways of living and being.

Truth and Wisdom flower,

spreading Beauty's grace to

all who recognize and serve with

labors of Love to help awaken

the nations and people to

the plight of the planet.

Each moment is precious!

For who has felt the subtle harmony

that radiates from a soul

peace-centered in Love?

Who has seen one little spark

ignite a dying ember

and set a faint heart

aglow with Fire?

An awakened heart pulsates

to the universal song: be it

of harmony and hope, or

be it discordant with pain.

Our heartbeats play their part,

throbbing in unity with Wisdom

and the unseen Choir of Love

in every precious moment.

Look to Wisdom.

She will lead you from

fear to freedom, and

liberate the imprisoned soul.

Our days are numbered;

too soon we vacate our

Earth-worn bodies.

Entering the portal to Love's unseen

Realm, will Wisdom hold sway; or

alas, must we return anew

to reap all we have sown, and for

further study of Her ways?

Wisdom drops her Veil; we are

wounded with yearning as

we sense the greater Life.

Mystery whispers our name.

Behold, O eternal soul!

New birth portends wider horizons,

heightened Being.

Bury the dry bones of yesterday.

Basking in solitude, Silence is

the Friend who stills

lurking desires, as

Wisdom cuts through tangled

webs of illusion.

Meditation lights the Flame.

Like many an ignored intention,

ephemeral were all our aspirations

when ego led the parade.

Children in all innocence know Wisdom.

They spontaneously express

a natural affinity for wisdom

with joy beyond many an elder's

imagination.

The humble learn from them.

The profane world hears not

the Voice of Wisdom;

while in the silent inner

Sanctum of our hearts, where

She dwells, our souls

glean Her whispered words

of love and good counsel;

She invites us to become peace,

to share our resources,

to offer justice to all,

to extend truth, and

to radiate joy.

Like us, Creation breathes in

pollution wrought by greed

through uncaring hearts

and minds.

To balance and heal Her horrific

wounds, Creation exerts Itself:

Nature's patterns shift;

disasters ensue that bring

devastation and death

to thousands in their wake.

Our children, whom we love,

and the generations to come,

will receive only a legacy

of lost hopes and dreams.

For what is not destroyed by

humanity's ignorance or disdain for

Nature's checks and balances, will

implode into plagues, further violence,

and a chaotic world gone awry.

O people of this planet,

O heads of world nations,

heed the Cry, the Call!

Times have never been so

dangerous or the stakes for

our survival so high.

Listen! Many now live among us

from the Realms of Love

to help guide us through illusion.

Silent be! *Listen* and heed!

Love and Wisdom see the crises

of these terrible times;

with Wisdom and Love

in the Oneness of all Being,

we can serve in the Divine Plan

to spiritualize our Home.

Hopes and dreams are renewed as

planet Earth, Herself,

is healed—holy and whole

once again.

Our wisdom is rooted and grows
In the pains and sorrows,
The blessings and gifts of life,
Where deep, abiding Love makes Its home.

Meditation Seventeen

Do you think that wayward

thoughts and actions

mean nothing?

Beware and Awaken!

For your every thought,

like a boomerang rebounds

inviting actions that

create self-fulfilling results.

Thoughts emanating from

hearts cleansed by

refining Fire are like arrows

that find the intended mark.

Most powerful are clear, focused

and loving thoughts that

extend out to awaken hearts,

while half-hearted thoughts

may only reach the few at hand.

Silence holds stray thoughts

at bay gently blessing others.

Remember, each thought is,

in a real sense, your prayer.

Awaken from the ignorance and illusions

of this, our wounded world;

they tend to paralyze us

with fear and apathy!

Open the door

to spiritual disciplines,

to the soul's song of

inner silence, the joy

we share on Wisdom's path.

Shatter the prison bars!

Heed not life's illusive

and fleeting pleasures,

worldly pursuits, addictions,

and attachments.

Myriad are the brilliant

soul flowers that bloom

as Wisdom is awakened

within each heart.

In deep meditation, that

blessed abode of Silence,

Wisdom sifts and scatters
the chaff for the flowering of
Divine Communion.
Cultivate Wisdom in your
soul's Sacred Garden.
Tried and true, yet
ever new,
Wisdom leads the way
to an abundant harvest,
to a fruitful Life
of peace and beauty.
An outstretched Hand
unseen by earthly eyes
reaches to ours,
ever ready to guide
the willing soul to
new vistas of Love.
Do not allow the vicissitudes
of life to blind you to your
true Purpose, or distract you
from your unique path.
For deep, abiding Love
makes Its home in
a centered heart;

gentle joy and peace

encourage a creative soul

ready and willing to serve.

Do not hide from those who await

in the Realm of Love,

hidden behind the Veil,

for a summons from you.

A helpful Hand will

lift you up. **Know** that

you are never alone!

Be wary of all the mind loves

lest an idol is held dear,

seeking misguided pleasure

to satisfy an empty desire.

Yet, nothing begets nothing.

Wisdom expresses one true Love

within the Heart of Everything:

ever present, eternal,

faithful Friend, indwelling in

everyone, in every space.

Dying to all the temptations

that veil this Love, one

garners a Heavenly grace:

the Peace of Love

in every place

the blessed Spirit

and Holy Wisdom lead.

An unlived life enslaved by fear
Holds potential gifts in abeyance;
Wisdom's way spawns peace
In heart, mind, and soul.
Choose Wisdom!

Meditation Eighteen

Worldly pollution, media,
and a plethora of other distractions
cloud the mirror of
a peaceful heart.
Solitude and silence are
powerful medicines
for the soul:
toxins are cleansed so our
spiritual eyes may see
clear reflections of the Divine.
Linger not too long; enter
a new life of Service as
a beacon of light to gently
guide without guiding.
Even strangers will smile
in the beams of your
clarity and wisdom
and begin to shine.

Sprouting from Wisdom come
seeds of Silence, that bear
fruit for future harvests of
sharing and selfless service.
Planted in human hearts,
healing and hope flower
with each loving act
of kindness and each offering
of heartfelt assurance and gratitude.
Planetary plentitude provides
more than enough for all
when shared with equity.
Listen! *Hear* and heed
Wisdom's Call.
The moment has arrived
for the transformation of
the planet in the
Great Plan of Light,
Love, and Power.
Sharing and Service foster
freedom, fearlessness, and
heartfelt fulfillment.
Let Wisdom pave the path.
Follow the road to

reconciliation; forgiveness
will foster peace, harmony,
friendship: blessings for All.
Follow the road to Sharing;
seeing the plight of another
as if seeing it as your own—
for it is.
Follow the road to Service; for
co-creating with Love and Wisdom
gives birth to beatitude and beauty—
songs of gratitude arise.
Reconciliation, sharing, service;
a sacred trinity to awaken humanity
to right action and relationship,
to forgiveness and unconditional love:
the interconnectedness of All.
Beware! An unlived life
enslaved by fear holds
potential gifts in abeyance.
Map out the terrain of
your unique spiritual journey
in the uncharted depths;
create your life story
to include new dimensions of

well-being and joy.

Let not guilt or ego become
the directors your life.

Remember, you are at the helm
of your own story, the director
and stage manager
of your life's odyssey.

Present yourself to Center Stage,
where your psyche holds sway;
where peace, unity,
and wisdom await just behind
the curtain for their cue
and call from you.

Between the scenes and acts
of your life surrender to
the Heart's prayer deep at
the Sacred Altar within.

The Beloved and Holy Wisdom
welcome your Homecoming
wherever you are, whatever you do.

You are never alone.

Thus, as the final curtain falls,
you will be in the Peace of All-Being.

Silent be and see.

If you knew the

sumptuous feast of Love

and Wisdom abiding within

your heart, would you settle

for mere crumbs of illusion?

Do not swallow food from a source

offering no nourishment;

rather, seek spiritual Food

that satisfies and listen

in the Silence for Wisdom's Voice.

Like rays of the sun

warming and nourishing

the Earth, so the food of Life

comes from Teachers and Masters

of the Unseen Realm to

guide and nourish a willing heart

into the sunlight of Love.

Your heart in tune with the

Heart of the World beats

in harmony with the

oneness and unity of all Life.

Come! Rend the Veil

that, like a mist, cloaks an

Infinite Reality beyond time.

Come! Let Wisdom fill

your heart and soul with the

peace and joy beyond understanding.

We come to know the power of Silence
In deep meditation; here,
True Wisdom emerges silently,
Rising up from the Mystery
Of the unseen Source within all.

Meditation Nineteen

Awaken, all who would sleep

in a dream-world.

Breathe deeply! *Radiant* Light

is being beamed from on high:

energies to revitalize

our body and soul.

No longer deny the gifts

bestowed upon you

to be shared with all

in service to bless the world.

Great will be your joy

as you offer your Self in

service to and with Wisdom

and the Beloved.

Your Purpose will reveal Itself

as you pursue the Way of Truth.

Teach what you learn.
Join the Dance of Life.

We are here in the world
for only a moment,
to discover and follow
our own unique Purpose,
to learn to love, share, and
serve in all we do,
coming and going through
the age-old Gates of
birth and death.
Strangers we may seem to be;
yet, our souls return
together again and again
throughout the ages
to evolve into our true Self,
until the lessons are complete,
until our Love is unconditional,
and we serve in the Oneness
that we are with all.
As we walk with Wisdom,
with Love by our side, and

learn of Her ways,

dedicated Service may

arise unbidden.

We come to know the power

of Silence in deep meditation;

we begin to teach by our

mere presence, radiating the

Peace beyond understanding.

We shine!

An open heart awakened to

beauty, balance, and truth

may begin to emanate beams

of radiant soul-light;

where thoughts without thinking

rise up to inspire the ready soul,

while unspoken words are heard

in our receptive Silence

heralding joy in the

unseen Realm of Love and

life beyond the unseen Veil.

Heavenly Life intersects life here,

a Oneness of strangers in

our midst gathered in

community, yet

denied by those who have

yet to see and know

that Love is their true Home.

Allow the busy sounds of life

to meld into the fullness

of pure Silence as

you go about your daily life.

Listen to your heart

beating in harmony with

the rhythm of the cosmos;

here, the one who prays becomes

a prayer without words.

This silent space is a conduit

for Wisdom's Voice of Love,

to be heard with spiritual ears.

Guidance is ever-present

to all who seek, ask, and listen,

to all who yearn to

follow Love's Will.

Blessed are all who surrender

themselves into

the One Heart and the One Mind;

they walk freely with Love and

Wisdom by their sides into

the fullness of All being.

And blessed are all

who live in Her Light:

our guiding soul star.

They imbue the whole world

with goodness, kindness, and hope.

Sophia is present as we learn to listen,
To be still and know.
Listen to Her gentle whispers as
Our world changes, as hope re-awakens.
Now is an opportune time
To be alive.

Meditation Twenty

O Sophia, You grace our lives

with your lightness of Being,

inviting us to find

delight, joy, beauty, play

and mystery in

celebration and praise of Life.

Guide us to harmony and balance,

to an alignment between

our inner and outer ways.

Strike a resonant chord in our

soul and spirit to awaken in us

a keener awareness and

a more sensitive mindfulness.

Surprise us with insight

that broadens our seeing

the Oneness and interconnectedness

we are with All.

For You, O Sophia, can meet

all challenges;

You see all that is hidden and

delight in impossibilities

that, through You,

suddenly seem possible.

You evoke laughter in us at

what in others might

bring but tears as we learn

to take ourselves lightly.

Trusting in your gentle guidance,

your clear teachings,

we receive your gifts of

grace, hope, and courage;

inspired and encouraged,

we feel more alive, and

ready to thrive.

Our gratitude and joy

overflows out to others.

Even though the madness

of the world may remain,

we live now in the world,

yet are not of it—

lighter and more enlightened.

You teach us to see the magnificence

of the little things in life,

beloved Sophia!

You are at home everywhere—

in common, ordinary spaces

as well as in the marketplace.

You sit at the threshold,

the Door of our heart,

waiting for us to bid You enter.

Then, as we welcome You

into our lives, we come

to know You as our Friend,

aware of every detail

of our lives.

You instruct us to look

with physical eyes and

to see with our spirit's eyes;

here, insights may come

to delight our souls,

to discover the majesty in

all living things,

the divinity of Creation.

How can we but rejoice?

In your perfect timing,

O Friend,

You break into the concourse,

the commerce of business,

surprising our world-weary hearts,

and lifting burdens that

weigh on our souls.

Lighten up, You caution.

Be like the fountain in

a beautiful garden,

spouting showers of

sun-sparkling splashes

of living water that

sound like joy and laughter.

How can we keep from smiling?

We are assured that, You,

O Sophia, are near.

To bless grieving souls,

You may guide them to beauty—

ever an uplifting source

of Love and Light.

Imagine an exquisite garden

fragrant with healing perfumes,

embracing you with visual treats

to behold that can but soothe

a heavy heart:

bluebells and gentian

and showy hibiscus,

daisies and clover

and hollyhocks dancing;

lilacs and roses,

comfrey and thyme; and

all hidden spaces where

nature-spirits reside.

Sophia will greet you there, too.

Listen to Sophia's gentle whispers.

Our world is changing,

hope is re-awakening.

Now is an opportune time

to be alive!

Sophia and the Beloved

are calling us to reach for

our deepest aspirations,

to share in inspired Service,

to create a new world together,

a healed sacred Planet—

pulsating with life, and whole.

O friends, join the Divine Dance!

Let Wisdom lead the way as

you enter a vibrant, new Life

of delight, joy, and love without end.

Welcome the challenges we all face

as we give birth to new Life,

new Joy, and Peace beyond

anything we've ever known.

Blessed are all who answer Their Call.

Suggested Reading

The New Oxford Annotated Bible: A New Standard Version with the Apocrypha, Michael D. Coogan (ed.), 3rd edition, New York: Oxford University Press, 2007.

Alice O. Howell, The Dove in the Stone: Finding the Sacred in the Commonplace, Wheaton, IL: Quest Books, 1988.

Kathleen M. O'Connor The Wisdom Literature, Collegeville, MN: Liturgical Press, 1988.

A portion of the proceeds from **Walking with Wisdom** will be donated to Friends of Silence, a non-profit organization.